AF270382

HIGH-STAKES HEISTS

HOBBY HEISTS

KENNY ABDO

Fly!
An Imprint of Abdo Zoom
abdobooks.com

abdobooks.com

Published by Abdo Zoom, a division of ABDO, P.O. Box 398166, Minneapolis, Minnesota 55439. Copyright © 2025 by Abdo Consulting Group, Inc. International copyrights reserved in all countries. No part of this book may be reproduced in any form without written permission from the publisher. Fly!™ is a trademark and logo of Abdo Zoom.

Printed in the United States of America, North Mankato, Minnesota.
052024
092024

THIS BOOK CONTAINS RECYCLED MATERIALS

Photo Credits: Alamy, AP Images, Getty Images, Shutterstock
Production Contributors: Kenny Abdo, Jennie Forsberg, Grace Hansen
Design Contributors: Candice Keimig, Neil Klinepier

Library of Congress Control Number: 2023948555

Publisher's Cataloging-in-Publication Data

Names: Abdo, Kenny, author.
Title: Hobby heists / by Kenny Abdo
Description: Minneapolis, Minnesota : Abdo Zoom, 2025 | Series: High-stakes heists | Includes online resources and index.
Identifiers: ISBN 9781098285722 (lib. bdg.) | ISBN 9781098286422 (ebook) | ISBN 9781098286774 (Read-to-me eBook)
Subjects: LCSH: Theft--Juvenile literature. | Hobbies--Juvenile literature. | Miscellaneous facts--Juvenile literature. | Stealing--Juvenile literature. | Robbery--Juvenile literature.
Classification: DDC 364.162--dc23

TABLE OF CONTENTS

HOBBY HEISTS

Hobbies are a fun and relaxing way to collect good memories. Some people collect toys or coins. Some collect food. And others collect trouble!

TAXI
AFA 00

THE PLOTTING

Collectors have a wide range of interests. Some collect materials that mean something to them. Others collect items that they can sell for more money in the future. Unfortunately, those items can be the targets of thieves!

During the 1990s, Beanie Babies were loved worldwide. One night, 60,000 of the cute collectibles were stolen from a warehouse. The heist was supposedly planned by 77-year-old Ben Perri.

THE SCORES

In 2005, a tasty heist was cooked up. With rope ladders and night-vision goggles, crooks broke into a warehouse in southern France. They took $100,000 worth of **black truffles**!

Thieves took the term "sticky fingers" to a whole new level in 2011. A team stole $18 million worth of maple syrup in Quebec. It is considered one of the largest thefts in Canadian history.

There was once a major maple syrup heist. In 2011 and 2012, the maple syrup market was isrupted by the "Great Canadian Maple Syrup Heist."
SYRUP CRIME!!
Nearly 3,000 tons of maple syrup valued at roughly $18 million were stolen from Quebec suppliers.

AMSTERDAM CHEESE
Amsterdam
Cheese Museum
All cheese ready
CHEESE MUSEUM
Cheese Museum

Someone cut the cheese, but it wasn't the Amsterdam Cheese Museum. The museum once displayed a **platinum** slicer covered in 220 diamonds. Valued at $28,000, the slicer was stolen in 2015.

In 2016, a truck carrying 20,000 lbs of cheese was stolen in Wisconsin. The loot was worth $46,000 of **fromage**! And that was just one of three cheese-related heists in Wisconsin that year!

Northern Californian **beekeepers** were stung by crime when hundreds of beehives worth nearly $1 million went missing. Luckily, a suspect was found in 2017 with 2,500 of the stolen hives.

Everyone has heard of train robberies. But model train heists can be just as big! In 2022, a trailer holding a 40-foot (12-m) long railroad model was stolen. The trailer was recovered a few towns over, but some miniatures were not.

In 2024, a man broke into a home that he'd been hired to do repairs on. He stole a stamp collection worth $400,000 and a car. After a high-speed chase with the police, the thief was finally **apprehended**.

THE GETAWAY

Enjoying hobbies and collecting unique items are great **pastimes**. But when hobbies turn to heists, collectors learn to keep their cherished items locked up.

2017 POKEMON SM PROMO   #SM78
CHAMPIONS FESTIVAL
WORLDS 17 - CHAMPION
NM - MT
8
46491393
TRAINER
Stadium
Champions Festival
Once during each player's turn, if that player has 6 Pokémon in play, they may heal 10 damage from each of their Pokémon.
CHAMPION
Tropical Tidal Wave
If heads, discard all Trainer opponent has in play. If tails, Trainer cards (excluding rds) you have in play.
10
63922621
1999 POKEMON GAME
CHARIZARD - HOLO
1ST EDITION
#4
MINT 9
0246090Z
Charizard
100
21

GLOSSARY

apprehended – when a person is arrested for a crime they have committed.

beekeeper – a person who owns and breeds bees, especially for their honey.

black truffle – a fungi used in food that is considered one of the most expensive foods to buy due to its difficulty to grow and find.

fromage – a French word meaning "cheese."

pastime – an activity people participate in for their enjoyment.

platinum – a precious, silver-white metal that is more valuable than gold.

ONLINE RESOURCES

Booklinks
NONFICTION NETWORK
FREE! ONLINE NONFICTION RESOURCES

To learn more about hobby heists, please visit **abdobooklinks.com** or scan this QR code. These links are routinely monitored and updated to provide the most current information available.

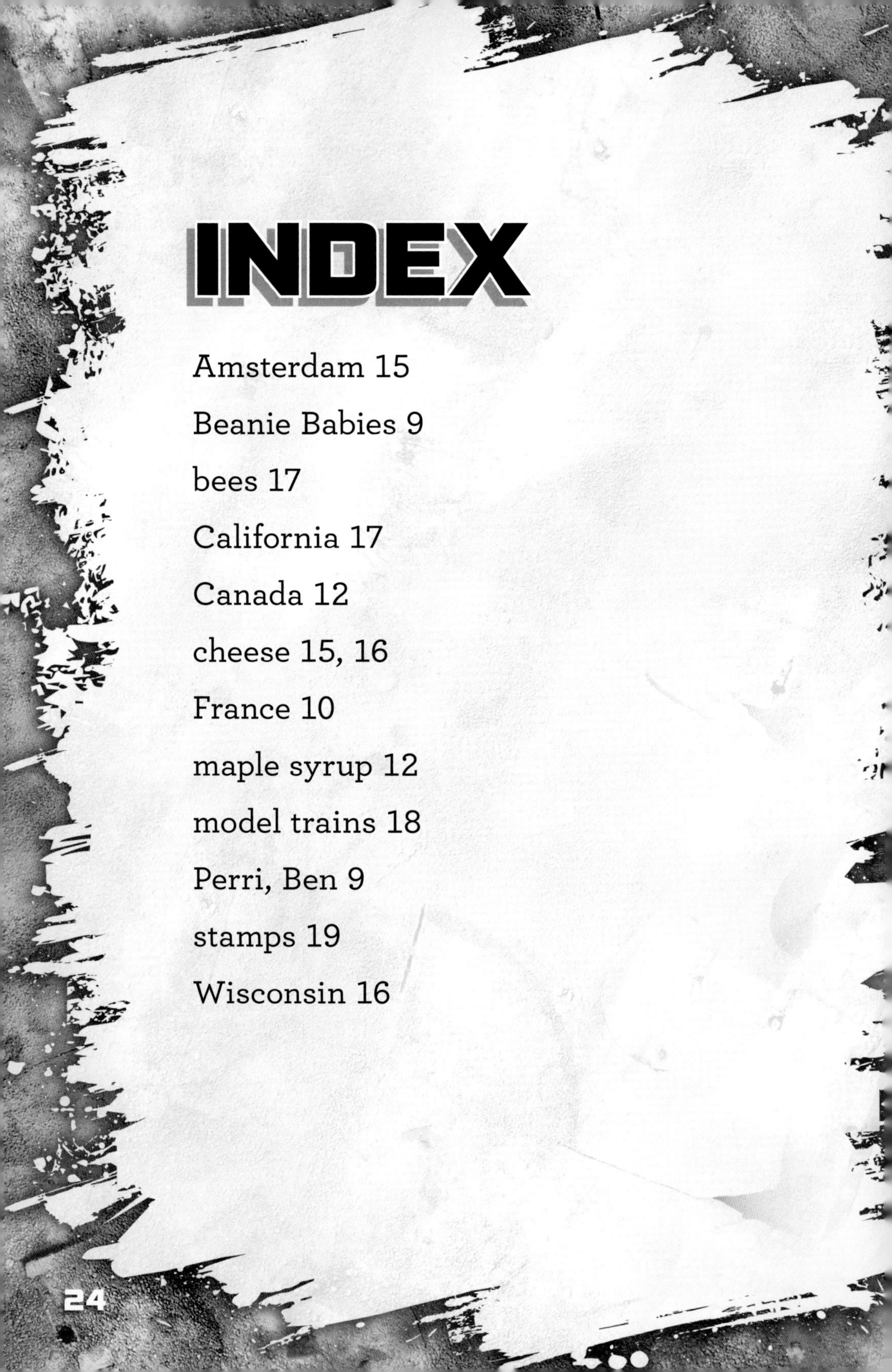

INDEX